A Special Gift

to: Courtney

from: Mrs. Arnold & Mrs. Miller

date: Nov. 21, 2004

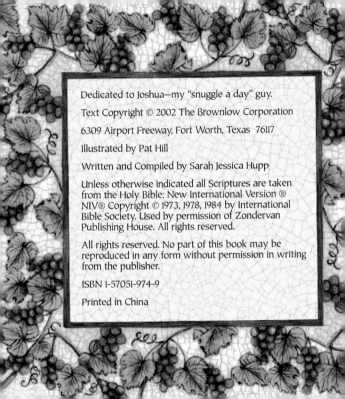

Dedicated to Joshua—my "snuggle a day" guy.

Text Copyright © 2002 The Brownlow Corporation

6309 Airport Freeway, Fort Worth, Texas 76117

Illustrated by Pat Hill

Written and Compiled by Sarah Jessica Hupp

Unless otherwise indicated all Scriptures are taken from the Holy Bible: New International Version ® NIV® Copyright © 1973, 1978, 1984 by International Bible Society. Used by permission of Zondervan Publishing House. All rights reserved.

ISBN 1-57051-974-9

Printed in China

Harvest of the Heart

LIVING THE FRUITFUL LIFE

Written and compiled by Sarah Jessica Hupp
Illustrated by Pat Hill

Brownlow

Little Treasures
Miniature Books

75 Ways to Spoil Your Grandchild
75 Ways to Be Good to Yourself
75 Ways to Calm Your Soul
75 Things to Do with a Friend
A Little Book of Blessing
A Little Book of Love
A Little Book for Tea Lovers
A Roof with a View
Baby's First Little Book
Baby Love
Baby Oh Baby

Catch of the Day
Dear Teacher
For My Secret Pal
Friends
The Gift of Friendship
Grandmother
Happiness Is Homemade
Happy Birthday
How Does Your Garden Grow
How to Be a Fantastic Grandmother
Love & Friendship
Mom
Sisters
Tea Time Friends
They Call It Golf

Introduction

"Ready for Picking" the sign declares.
It's blueberry season along the coast.
The bushes are full, and so are the baskets
of all who stop. By the end of the day, you
can tell who's lingered the longest by their
blue-tinged smiles.

Within these pages you'll find fresh fruit too.
Linger a while. Savor the taste. Leave with a
love-tinged smile, for the *Harvest of the Heart*
is ripe and ready for picking!

S.M.H.

The fruit of the Spirit
is love, joy, peace,
patience, kindness,
goodness, faithfulness,
gentleness and
self-control.
Against such things
there is no law.

GALATIANS 5:22-23

Love

What does love look like? It has
the hands to help others. It has the
feet to hasten to the poor and needy.
It has the eyes to see misery and want.
It has the ears to hear the sighs and
sorrows of men.
That is what love looks like.

SAINT AUGUSTINE

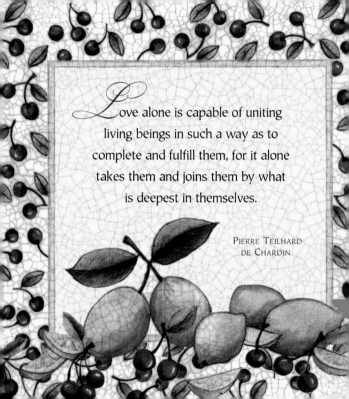

*L*ove alone is capable of uniting
living beings in such a way as to
complete and fulfill them, for it alone
takes them and joins them by what
is deepest in themselves.

PIERRE TEILHARD
DE CHARDIN

Love is patient, love is kind.
It does not envy, it does
not boast, it is not proud.
It is not rude, it is not self-
seeking, it is not easily angered,
it keeps no record of wrongs.
Love does not delight in evil
but rejoices with the truth.

1 CORINTHIANS 13:4-6

*C*hildren are underrated philosophers.
When several pre-schoolers were asked
to define "love," by far the most profound
definition came from a little girl who answered,
"Love is someone reading you your favorite
bedtime story. True love is not skipping any pages."

The hidden meaning:
To show someone you love them,
take time to do something that they want to do—
and take the time to do it right!

S.M.H.

*T*rue love is not only at the tongue's end,
but at the finger's end; it is the labor of love.

THOMAS WATSON

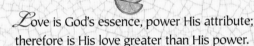

*L*ove is God's essence, power His attribute;
therefore is His love greater than His power.

RICHARD GARNETT

*L*ove is all we have,
the only way that each
can help the other.

EURIPIDES

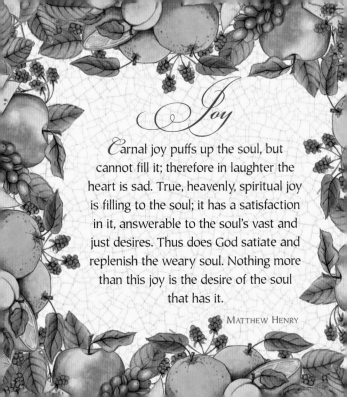

Joy

Carnal joy puffs up the soul, but cannot fill it; therefore in laughter the heart is sad. True, heavenly, spiritual joy is filling to the soul; it has a satisfaction in it, answerable to the soul's vast and just desires. Thus does God satiate and replenish the weary soul. Nothing more than this joy is the desire of the soul that has it.

MATTHEW HENRY

We miss the really great joys
of life scrambling for
bargain-counter happiness.

ROY L. SMITH

Be joyful always.

1 THESSALONIANS 5:16

Joy can only be multiplied when it is divided.

S.M.H.

The word "joy" is too great and grand to be confused with the superficial things we call happiness.

KIRBY PAGE

Joyful, joyful, we adore Thee,
God of glory, Lord of love;
Hearts unfold like flowers before Thee,
Opening to the sun above.
Melt clouds of sin and sadness;
Drive the dark of doubt away;
Giver of immortal gladness,
Fill us with the light
of day!

HENRY VAN DYKE

Peace

The fruit of righteousness will be peace; the effect
of righteousness will be quietness and confidence forever.

ISAIAH 32:17

All men desire peace, but very few desire
those things that make for peace.

THOMAS À KEMPIS

There's a peace in my heart that
the world never gave,
A peace it can not take away;
Tho' the trials of life
may surround like a cloud,
I've a peace that has come
there to stay!

ANNE S. MURPHY

When you have found confidence
and rest that God is who He says He is,
that He'll do everything He says He'll do,
you have found true peace.

J. RODRIGUEZ

Peace within makes beauty without.

GEORGE HERBERT

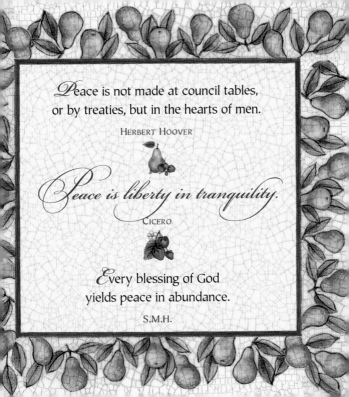

*P*eace is not made at council tables,
or by treaties, but in the hearts of men.

HERBERT HOOVER

Peace is liberty in tranquility.

CICERO

*E*very blessing of God
yields peace in abundance.

S.M.H.

Peace is one of those things, like happiness, which we are sure to miss if we aim at them directly.

DOROTHY L. SAYERS

Seek peace and pursue it.

PSALM 34:14

Patience

*H*ave patience with all things, but
chiefly have patience with yourself.
Do not lose courage in considering
your own imperfections, but instantly
set about remedying them—every day
begin the task anew.

ST. FRANCIS DE SALES

*Waiting time is never wasted time,
for patience is a key to contentment.*

S.M.H.

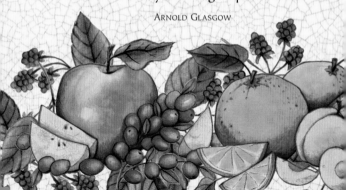

*The key to everything is patience.
You get the chicken by hatching the egg,
not by smashing it open.*

ARNOLD GLASGOW

Wait for the LORD; be strong and take heart
and wait for the LORD.

PSALM 27:14

Please be patient. God isn't finished with me yet.

*P*atience strengthens the spirit,
sweetens the temper, stifles anger,
subdues pride, and bridles the tongue.

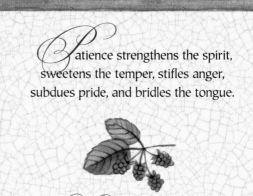

A man may at times be called
to do his duty by doing nothing, to work
by keeping still, to serve by waiting.

GEORGE MATHESON

Kindness

The greatest thing a man can do
for his heavenly Father is to be kind
to some of His other children.

<small>HENRY DRUMMOND</small>

Kindness always pays, but it pays most
when you do not do it for pay.

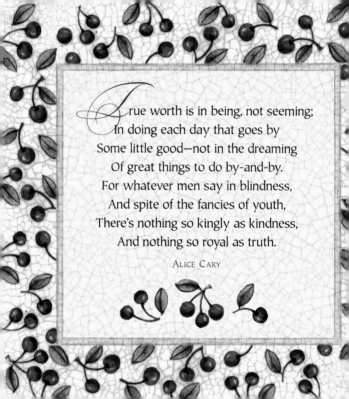

True worth is in being, not seeming;
In doing each day that goes by
Some little good—not in the dreaming
Of great things to do by-and-by.
For whatever men say in blindness,
And spite of the fancies of youth,
There's nothing so kingly as kindness,
And nothing so royal as truth.

ALICE CARY

Make sure that nobody
pays back wrong for wrong, but
always try to be kind to each other
and to everyone else.

1 Thessalonians 5:15

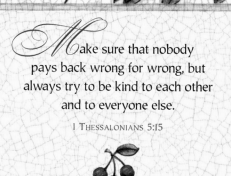

Kindness is loving people
more than they deserve.

Joseph Joubert

*K*ind words toward those you daily meet,
Kind words and actions right,
Will make this life of ours most sweet,
Turn darkness into light.

ISAAC WATTS

*Compassion will cure more sins
than condemnation.*

HENRY WARD BEECHER

Goodness

Do all the good you can

By all the means you can

In all the ways you can

In all the places you can

At all the times you can

To all the people you can

As long as you ever can!

JOHN WESLEY

That which is striking and
beautiful is not always good,
but that which is good is
always beautiful.

NINON DE L'ENCLOS

The fruit of the light consists in all
goodness, righteousness and truth.

EPHESIANS 5:9

Goodness is something so simple: always live for others, never to seek one's advantage.

DAG HAMMERSKJOLD

*G*oodness consists not in the outward things we do, but in the inward thing we are.

*G*reatness is not found in possessions, power, position, or prestige. It is discovered in goodness, humility, service, and character.

Faithfulness

Is your place a small place?
Tend it with care!—He set you there.
Is your place a large place?
Guard it with care!—He set you there.
Whate'er your place, it is
Not yours alone, but his
Who set you there.

JOHN OXENHAM

The word of the Lord
is right and true; he is faithful
in all he does.

PSALM 33:4

Faithfulness in little things is a big thing.

ST. JOHN
CHRYSOSTOM

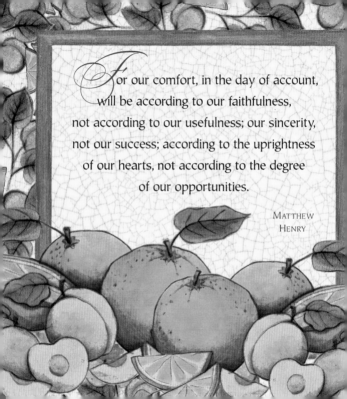

*F*or our comfort, in the day of account, will be according to our faithfulness, not according to our usefulness; our sincerity, not our success; according to the uprightness of our hearts, not according to the degree of our opportunities.

MATTHEW HENRY

Some trees are quick to blossom in the spring, but others take their time.
When it appears that we are awaiting a late blooming promise from God, wait for it.
God is faithful to his promises.
He will surely bring it to pass.

S.M.H.

Faithfulness is being true to our beliefs and commitments even when others are falling away.

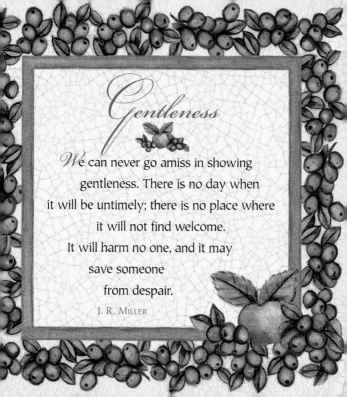

Gentleness

We can never go amiss in showing gentleness. There is no day when it will be untimely; there is no place where it will not find welcome. It will harm no one, and it may save someone from despair.

J. R. MILLER

Three principles of gentleness:

There is nothing stronger than
God's gentleness.

Power melded with gentleness will
accomplish more than intimidation
and violence.

You are kind to yourself when
you are gentle with others.

S.M.H.

*M*ake a rule and pray to God to help
you to keep it, never, if possible, to lie down
at night without being able to say:
"I have made one human being at least a little wiser,
or a little happier, or at least a little better this day."

<small>CHARLES KINGSLEY</small>

Let your gentleness be evident to all.

The Lord is near.

PHILIPPIANS 4:5

Feelings are everywhere—be gentle.

J. MASAI

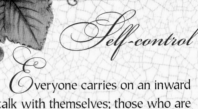

Self-control

Everyone carries on an inward talk with themselves; those who are self-controlled have learned not to answer back in anger, knowing that the one who conquers himself is braver than the one who conquers his enemies.

S.M.H.

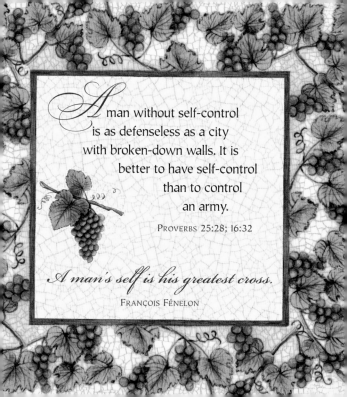

A man without self-control is as defenseless as a city with broken-down walls. It is better to have self-control than to control an army.

Proverbs 25:28; 16:32

A man's self is his greatest cross.

François Fénelon

Living the fruitful life means living with the knowledge that there is something more important than our life.